MW01280141

GOD BLESS

You

Bro Tony

PSALM
119:105

PUBLISHED *by*
PARABLES
Earthly Stories with a Heavenly Meaning

Anthony Ritthaler

Amazing Grace
A Life Sheltered By God

PUBLISHED *by* PARABLES
Earthly Stories with a Heavenly Meaning

Pathways To The Past

Each volume stands alone as an Individual Book
Each volume stands together with others
to enhance the value of your collection

Build your Personal, Pastoral or Church Library
Pathways To The Past contains an ever-expanding list of
Christendom's most influencial authors

Augustine of Hippo
Athanasius
E. M. Bounds
John Bunyan
Brother Lawrence
Jessie Penn-Lewis
Bernard of Clairvaux
Andrew Murray
Watchman Nee
Arthur W. Pink
Hannah Whitall Smith
R. A. Torrey
A. W. Tozer
Jean-Pierre de Caussade
Thomas Watson
And many, many more.

————————————————————

Amazing Grace
Anthony Ritthaler
    Rights: All Rights Reserved
    ISBN 978-1-945698-53-8
    Doctrinal theology, Inspiration
    Salvation, Meditation
    Other books by this author include: Walking On The Water With Jesus
(Volume 1 and 2), Soaring With Eagles (Volume 1 and 2), Roaring At The Enemy,
A Devil From The Beginning and Escaping Depression: A Book Of Hope, Help And
Healing

Cover Design by Fury Cover Design
www.furycoverdesign.com

ANTHONY RITTHALER

AMAZING GRACE
A LIFE SHELTERED BY GOD

PUBLISHED *by* PARABLES
Earthly Stories with a Heavenly Meaning

TABLE OF CONTENTS

SPECIAL THANKS

With a book of this nature I want to first of all thank the Lord Almighty for constantly sending His angels to watch over this unworthy sinner. I'm truly humbled beyond degree for His watch care and His love, and it overwhelms me whenever I dwell on it for any length of time. The pages of my life have been covered with shelter from Above and I've always been grateful for it. Without the unseen hand of God's grace we are all helpless and headed for a life of danger.

God Almighty has brought me through storms, battles, hardships, accidents, threats, afflictions, and near-death experiences all to show me His power and my inabilities in every way without Him. God's understanding is infinite. His love is impossible to comprehend, and his Spirit is able to perform miracles that are unimaginable. Thank you, Lord, for showing compassion on me for without you I'm nothing, and I will always remember that. Lord I love you with all that is in me.

Secondly, I want to send a very special thank you to my praying parents. As a child I would walk into my parents' room and find my dear mother praying for my safety and my soul and it impacted me as a young boy. My parents have constantly prayed for me all my life and because of it my steps have been ordered by the Lord. Through their prayers, mountains have been moved on my behalf, spiritually speaking, and our relationship with each other has always been strong. I believe I'm a blessed man today because I've always tried to honor my parents with respect, love, and appreciation and God is pleased with anyone who has this mindset. Thanks Mom and Dad for your prayers, support and love for Jesus Christ.

Last of all, I would like to thank God's Holy Spirit that has guided me for most of my life. You have been my compass, my light, my friend, and my greatest support of all. Thank you for remaining inside me in a dark and uncertain world and thanks for being there through the good times and the bad times. Without your overshadowing I would not be here, and I thank you from the depths of my soul. Jesus, you truly are a friend that sticketh closer than a brother. Thank you for your amazing grace that rescues mankind.

INTRODUCTION

As we all reflect back over the pages of our life we will discover moments ordained by the Hand of God and they had nothing to do with luck. There are Moments of Divine appointments that leave us in amazement and wonder over what just happened.

We can all give stories of God's amazing grace in our lives and in this book, I want to highlight times where God, in his Mercy, spared me from danger and even death as only he could. We serve a God that does everything on purpose and nothing just happens. God has a master design for everything that takes place in our lives and His ways are past finding out.

In this book, we will look at amazing moments in my life that point to the sovereign mercy of Almighty God. The God we serve can do the impossible and everything about Him is nothing short of amazing. From the time of my youth until this present moment, God has been my guide, my helper, and my friend. As we look at these stories to come I hope all of us realize that God loves us, and He has a plan for us. Each story will bless you, and it will show just how merciful God really is.

My life has been filled with times of extreme danger and I've watched how God has sheltered me and kept me safe through them all. All the glory goes to God for without Him we could do nothing. This book will prove to anyone that God is real, and I trust that it opens our eyes to how God protects His children. Many will relate to this book because I know you have your own stories as well. Let's give God the praise He deserves because without His amazing grace none of us would be here. Allow these stories to touch you and open your eyes to the fact that the Lord wants to do great things with all of us. The fact that we are still alive is clear proof that He wants to use us for His honor and glory.

Many today call God's miracles "God Moments" because it's times in our lives where everything points back to God Above. My goal in writing these stories is that everything said and done with these times in my life clearly point back to a thrice Holy God. We serve a God of power, strength, love, and grace. God's grace is a beautiful thing and we need to remember all the times in our lives when God showed mercy and grace upon us.

This book will take you on a journey through my life where God saved me from death, kept me from harm, and sent His angels to watch over me. It will amaze you how many times God has stepped in during my young life and I pray that it will dawn on us just how amazing His grace really is. The Bible says in Isaiah 54:17, That no weapon formed against us shall prosper and when we'll walk close to the Master we can experience protection and safety. If God can walk through the fire with three Hebrew children and shut the mouths of the lions for Daniel, He can work miracles for you.

These stories will shed a light on God's mercy, His love, and His grace in a great way. All praise and honor goes to God and I'm trusting God to bless you through these upcoming stories, and may God's Blessed Holy Spirit encourage you through this book. What an amazing God we serve.

Scripture Introduction

Isaiah 54:17 No man that is formed against thee shall prosper.

Psalm 90:9 For all our days are passed away in thy wrath; we spend our years as a tale that is told.

ANTHONY RITTHALER

CHAPTER ONE

THE AMAZING GRACE OF THE LORD ABOVE

Every blessing and every miracle is from Above, but some seem to stand out more than others. The Bible says that the "Goodness of God leadeth men to repentance" and this story brings me to my knees whenever I dwell on it.

The magnitude of this miracle is breathtaking, and I stand before you this day as a byproduct of the Grace of God. Jesus is the giver of life and the giver of strength and without His touch upon my body I would surely be bedridden today. Isaiah 40:29 says. "He giveth power to the faint: and to them that have no might He increaseth strength". Often in my life God has reached down from Heaven and touched my back and He has performed miracles on several different occasions. The power of prayer has been the key for me and the only reason I'm still walking today is because God has allowed it to happen.

This next story staggers me and brings me to tears because it's a prime example of what God is able to do.

May the Lord richly bless you through this story.

For anyone who knows me personally you understand that my back is not the strongest. Between the step in my back as a baby and the many injuries I've encountered, it's a blessing that I'm still standing today. God has been extremely kind towards me and has given me the grace to keep moving on.

About 8 years ago, while working at my job, twelve signs fell on top of me with a lot of force and in total it was over 1,400 pounds of weight. When it happened, I had no time to react and I fell beneath the heavy load. Once my coworker realized this happened he ran to my rescue and piled off the signs as fast as he could, but the damage had been done. This accident would have killed most but thanks to God's help I was back to work the very next day. A week later, I walked down the wedding aisle without even a limp and married my dear wife. The old song says, "Isn't the love of Jesus something wonderful". The theme of my life has been mercy, grace, and healing from Above. My mom says I'm her miracle and all I can say is thank you to the Lord Above.

I'll end this chapter with this verse because it fits this chapter perfectly.

Ephesians 3:20 "Now, unto Him that is able to do exceeding abundantly above all that we ask or think, according to the power that worketh in us".

Scriptures For This Chapter

Isaiah 40:29 He giveth power to the faint: and to them that have no might He increaseth strength.

Ephesians 3:20 Now, unto Him that is able to do exceeding abundantly above all that we ask or think, according to the power that worketh in us.

Psalm 37:4 "Delight thyself also in the Lord; and He shall give thee the desires of thine heart."

Isaiah 1:19 "If ye be willing and obedient, ye shall eat the good of the land:"

Matthew 6:33 "But seek ye first the kingdom of God, and His righteousness: and all these things shall be added unto you."

ANTHONY RITTHALER

CHAPTER 2

IT COULD HAVE BEEN ME THAT DAY

Sometimes we don't even realize it but we are standing on the brink of disaster. Many times, we are just a few feet away from tragedy and without God's mercy we are helpless in those moments. Every time we get in a vehicle or go out in public we have little control over what can happen next. Life is unpredictable and unstable at best. Anything can happen at any given time and we must be alert and aware of our surroundings. If a bomb were to go off or a car cut in front of us or lightning hit us we would be powerless against such things. Many have stood in line at a store and the person next to them dropped dead of a heart attack. Tragedy can strike at any time and every day is a gift from our Maker.

We have no power over how God works, and life is unexplainable. Moments happen that grab our attention, and everything happens for a reason. The next story is clear in my mind and it no doubt caused me to pay more attention to every detail of life. This moment happened three feet from me and I could have been the one rushed to the E.R. that day. Allow this story to grab your attention and remind you just how close danger is to all of us.

Back in the year 2000, I had the great joy of going to the Buick Open with dear friends to watch the greatest golfers in the world play up close and personal. As a young man it was amazing to me to follow the best and learn from their every move. As the day wore on, I snuck away from the crowd and followed the greatest golfer in the world for about 6 holes. As we arrived on the 10th hole, a long par 5, I got down to about three hundred yards from the tee shot guessing where the ball might land. After a long pause, the great golfer hit his shot, and the ball stayed in the air for what seemed like an eternity. Standing right next to me was a woman talking with her friend and I could see the ball coming quickly our way. When the ball arrived, it hit this dear woman in the head and went about 20 feet in the air and immediately she fell to the ground. There was blood everywhere and the lady fell to the ground lifeless and she was rushed to the hospital.

To this day I have no clue what happened to her, but it happened 3 feet from me and it could have been me. The Bible teaches us to prepare to meet thy God and this woman was not prepared. When I look back on this moment It's a reminder of two things: first we must always be prepared, and secondly we must always be aware that without God's mercy we would not be here. So often we stand on the edge of disaster and it's because of Grace we make it through. Please don't ever forget that. Proverbs 27:1 says, "Boast not thyself of tomorrow, for thou knowest not what a day may bring forth".

Scriptures For This Chapter

Proverbs 27:1 Boast not thyself of tomorrow, for thou knowest not what a day may bring forth.

James 1:17 Every good gift and every perfect gift cometh from Above

ANTHONY RITTHALER

CHAPTER 3

NO WEAPON THAT IS FORMED AGAINST THEE SHALL PROSPER

Whenever you venture out to warn a dark world of their wicked ways you can expect a battle. The Christian life is not a picnic, and the devil's crowd greatly outnumbers God's crowd. When we bring the Light to a lost world all hell can break loose and anything can happen. As God's children we need not to fear because John 4:4 says, "Greater is He that is in you, than he that is in the world". Everywhere we go with God's Word, God goes with us and although danger may be all around God can set our feet on solid ground. Timothy 1:7 says, "For God hath not given us the Spirit of fear, but of power, and of love, and of a sound mind". Isaiah 41:10 says, "fear thou not; for I am with thee: Be not dismayed for I am thy God: I will strengthen thee, yea I will help thee; yea I will uphold thee with the right hand of My righteousness". Although Satan will rise up people to stand in our way, God will make sure we achieve what we set out to do.

Through the years of knocking on doors telling others about Christ we have seen many strange things and faced a few death threats, but God has stood by our side every step of the way. On two separate occasions I've had guns pulled on me that threatened my life, but God watched over me both times. The famous verse in Isaiah 54:17 says this, "No weapon that is formed against Thee shall prosper". This verse has been so true in my life and we have a promise from God that He will never leave us nor forsake us. Throughout my life Isaiah 54:17 has come to pass time and time again and to feel God's presence is what life is all about.

To all the Saints of God who may read this I encourage you to tell the world of Jesus with total confidence and without fear because God will stand by your side. If God can protect me there is no reason why he can't protect you. Always remember, our mission on earth is to shine as lights in the darkness and with God's help we can do anything. Both times the weapons were pulled on me I was free from all fear and that is because God was nearby.

This chapter is just another example of God's grace in my life and it's humbling to say the least. God has kept me alive for a reason and I want to make my short time on earth count for His honor and glory.

May we all understand that we have a purpose and if we are still here we must find out what our purpose is and get busy accomplishing it. Thank God for this wonderful statement "No weapon that is formed against you shall prosper". God is our great protector and without him we can do nothing.

Scriptures For This Chapter

I John 4:4 Greater is He that is in you, than he that is in the world.

II Timothy 1:7 For God hath not given us the spirit of fear, but of power, and of love, and of a sound mind

ANTHONY RITTHALER

CHAPTER 4

JESUS TOOK THE WHEEL

The faster we learn that we are not in control of our lives, but God is, the more at ease we will be. We must all allow God to grab the steering wheel of our life and drive us where we need to go. When God is directing our lives, we will always arrive at our destination. The old song says, "Jesus Savior pilot me" and this must be our attitudes while we sojourn through life. With Jesus in the driver's seat we can relax and be at peace because he knows the way better than we ever could. Job 23:10 says, "But he knoweth the way that I take: When he hath tried me, I shall come forth as gold". The only hope anyone has of becoming a precious jewel is to get out of the way and allow God to take us where we need to go. As we travel through life God can protect us from any danger that lurks, and this next story will prove just that. Allow God's Spirit to bless you with this story.

Around ten years ago while on my way to Cedar Point something happened suddenly to me that nearly ended my life. Everything was going smooth. I was praising God, singing his praises when all of a sudden, my truck started shaking out of control and like a magnet it was taking me across three lanes of traffic. Parking that truck felt like landing a plane as my tire completely blew out and I lost control of my truck. God completely took over and grabbed my steering wheel and somehow guided me safely to the side of the freeway. I avoided many cars and also avoided flipping my car over as God's presence filled my truck. As the truck came to a stop I remember pausing and thanking God for what he just did.

Anything could have happened in that moment, but God stepped in and took the wheel that day. I'm still amazed by His Grace in this situation and without His presence on that day I would not be here today. We serve a powerful Long-suffering God.

28

Scriptures For This Chapter

Job 23:10 But he knoweth the way that I take: When he hath tried me, I shall come forth as gold.

ANTHONY RITTHALER

CHAPTER 5

A WALL OF DEFENSE IN THE MIDDLE OF THE NIGHT

Throughout the pages of God's Word there is a constant theme of the Lord protecting those who fear Him. When Daniel was in the lion's den God sent his angel to give every lion lock jaw and no harm was done to God's man. When the three Hebrew children were cast into the fiery furnace the Bible says not a single hair was burnt and God walked with them through the fire.

Seemly, every where you travel through the inspired Word of God you find God sending his angels to protect those who serve Him. David said this in Psalm 18:2 "The Lord is my rock, and my deliverer; my God, my strength, in whom I trust; my buckler, and the horn of my salvation, and my high tower". Psalm 91: 2-4 says, "I will say of the Lord, He is my refuge and my fortress; my God; in Him will I trust. Surely, He shall deliver thee from the snare of the fowler, and from the noisome pestilence, He shall cover thee with His feathers and under his wings shalt they trust His truth shall be his shield and buckler".

Wherever the child of God goes the Bible teaches that God is able to set up a wall of defense on their behalf. The Bible declares in Psalm 4:3, "But know that the Lord hath set apart Him that is Godly for Himself". In other words, there is a special place at His table for those who walk in truth. The Bible says this in Psalm 34:7, "The angel of the Lord encampeth round about them that fear Him; and delivereth them". For those who fear God the Bible teaches that a personal angel from on high will be assigned to watch over them. The Bible declares that a hedge was set up around Job and the devil could not get past that wall of defense unless God gave him the ok to do so. When we walk close to Jesus He will assign personal bodyguards called angels to keep us safe. The next story is just another example of God's grace, mercy, and protection sent to me in my time of need. We serve a wonderful merciful God and I pray this story reveals God's grace once again.

Years ago, I was invited to my pastor's house in Detroit to watch the NBA finals Game 2 between the Los Angeles Lakers and the Detroit Pistons and it was a long night and I was tired. In those days I was working sixty five hours a week doing a very physical construction job and the game went till 2:30 in the morning. While driving on the freeway that night at around 3:00AM my eyes became real heavy and I fell asleep at the wheel. My truck began to shake, and I found myself on the side of I-94 one inch from the ditch. Next to me was two damaged construction barrels from the company I worked for and I praised God that night for God's mercy in allowing them to be there. If not for these barrels being a wall of defense I would have went into a deep ditch at seventy miles per hour and would probably not be here today. God allowed me to place those same barrels on that freeway earlier in the day and they saved my life later that night. God, in His infinite wisdom, love, and grace seen up the road a bit and sent a wall of defense to shield me from death that night and all glory goes to the Lord.

Sometimes we fail to realize how close we are to danger and if not for grace none of us would be here today. The old songwriter said, "Through many dangerous toils and snares I have already come, but grace shall lead me home". Thank God for grace for without it we would be of all men most miserable.

Scriptures For This Chapter

Psalm 18:2 The Lord is my rock, and my deliverer; my God, my strength, in whom I trust; my buckler, and the horn of my salvation, and my high tower.

Psalm 4:3 But know that the Lord hath set apart Him that is Godly for Himself.

CHAPTER 6

GOD SHOWED MERCY ON A COLD OCTOBER DAY

Probably the greatest gift we can possess along with God's gift of salvation is the gift of good health. Thousands are born each year with health problems and if you have great health you ought to praise God for it. Some are born with a bad heart, while others are born with only one kidney. Some are born with body parts missing and others have afflictions that plague them on a daily basis. If you wake up every morning with two arms, two legs, two eyes, and good health you should thank God for that because everyone is not that lucky.

I've never taken for granted the health God has blessed me with and I'm humbled beyond measure for it. Whenever I see folks with one leg, or one hand, my heart hurts for them because I am aware of the fact it could very well be me. In Luke 17 we read of the lepers that begged God for healing and thank God the Lord showed mercy and healed them. Often in the Bible you find the handicapped and the crippled desperately begging God for help because it's no fun to live in that condition. I'm very humbled by good health and the next story will magnify the mercy of God in a great way.

God has been gracious towards me throughout my life and it's a miracle that I'm an author today. Once you read this story you will understand why. Enjoy this story and as you read this think how amazing God's grace really is.

On a cold windy October day in Jackson, Michigan a miracle took place that I praise God for every day. At the time it was not delightful but as time has gone on and I reflect back on it I'm grateful because it could have been far worse. Me and a man named Mark were working on the side of the freeway and I was holding a stub in place while he was using a jack hammer that could go through concrete. What Mark would do is lift the jack hammer in the air and slam it over the stub and hammer it into the ground, so we could attach a sign to it and it would hold the sign in place. As we were nearing the end of our work day I was holding the stub in place, but my right hand was too high, and he slammed the hammer on my hand and hammered away. For over 4 seconds he hammered away before he noticed my finger was trapped under there. Immediately my nail turned purple and the pain was intense. The nail fell off and I had to go to the hospital.

Somehow, I kept that finger and in about 4 days it healed up and within a month the nail grew back and now I have no problems at all. I've now written 9 books and through God's grace my hand is as good as new. Psalm 26:7 says, "That I may publish with the voice of thanksgiving and tell of all thy wonderous works". It's amazing that I still have my thumb because that jack hammer cuts through anything and it weighed about 75 pounds. When I look at my hand today I cannot tell anything ever happened and I must conclude God is the major reason why. Psalm 86:10 says, "For thou art great, and doest wonderous things, thou art God alone". We serve a compassionate loving savior and every day I stand amazed by what he can do.

Scriptures For This Chapter

Psalm 86:10 For thou art great, and doest wonderous things, thou art God alone.

Psalm 26:7 That I may publish with the voice of thanksgiving and tell of all thy wonderous works.

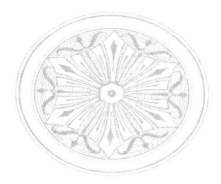

CHAPTER 7

INCHES FROM DISASTER

When we get to glory and God reveals all the many times He sheltered us from harm, I believe we will fall on our face and thank Him from the depths of our soul. On earth we will never be able to see with natural eyes how God moves behind the scenes of our lives but in Heaven we will have perfect understanding. Our gracious redeemer is always looking out for our good and He directs our pathways in the ways of righteousness and He leads us away from danger. If we serve God and choose to do His will nothing will be able to stop us with His help. Psalm 20:7 says "Some trust in chariots, and some in horses: but we will remember the name of the Lord our God".

The Lord is our shelter and with His strength he will shield us from the enemy. God is able to deliver his Saints from all trouble and He can send Divine protection in our time of need. The Bible still says in Psalm 46:10, "God is our refuge and strength, a very present help in trouble". In our greatest times of testing and need, Jesus is that friend that sticketh closer than a brother and this next story will prove just that. Enjoy this story and I trust it will bring glory to our risen Christ.

Early one morning I turned on the TV and in Michigan that morning there were over 42 accidents reported and the conditions were extremely dangerous. Black ice was everywhere, and I've never drove in weather like that and it was scary. Back in those days I was driving an S-10 pick-up and it was a bit hard to control that little truck and before I knew it I was spinning out of control. My truck spun three times before landing safely in a ditch face first. As I was sitting in that ditch I looked on either side of me and there was a tree on the right and a mailbox on the left and I was in between them both.

On my radio that morning I was listening to a song about Heaven and I did not get out of my truck until I was done with that song. My mind was on Heaven that day and the damaged truck meant nothing to me. Once again, I walked out of that accident without a single scar and although my truck was messed up my spirit was lifted to the Heavens. Anything could have happened to me that morning but because the night before I gave a dear preacher 1,500 dollars I believe God spared my life. God will provide protection to anyone whose heart is set towards serving Him.

As folks drove by that day and seen my truck in the ditch and me praising God they thought I was nuts but if they could have felt the presence of God that morning they would have been shouting too. I'll never take for granted the Hand of God in every situation and if you would have seen my truck that day there would be no way you would have thought someone could have walked out of there without being hurt. However I'm here testifying of God's mercy and declaring that I had no hurt at all.

God is so very good to all of us and right now we should all lift up Holy Hands to our great Savior. The Bible says this in Psalm 145:8, "The Lord is gracious, and full of compassion: slow to anger and of great mercy". To that verse and many more I say Amen and Amen.

Scriptures For This Chapter

Psalm 20:7 Some trust in chariots, and some in horses: but we will remember the name of the Lord our God.

Psalm 46:10 God is our refuge and strength, a very present help in trouble.

CHAPTER 8

THE CROOKED SHALL BE MADE STRAIGHT

As we travel through the pages of God's Word, we read about amazing miracles that bless our souls. God is able to do anything, and nothing is beyond his capabilities. The Bible makes this statement in Luke 3:5, "And the crooked shall be made straight". For years people have been calling me the walking miracle and it all goes back to the miracle I experienced when I was a baby.

Through the years I've had a lot of injuries and I should not be walking today. Every day I get out of bed I rejoice in the healing power of God and my mind often travels back to the miracle God performed for me many years ago. The following story will show just what God can do for those who pray with a heart of faith. Allow God to bless you through this story.

Shortly after being born, my dear parents discovered that there was something wrong with my spine, so they sought physicians. Immediately X-rays were run, and the results were not good at all. The doctor told my parents

I had a very rare step in my spine and out of fifty known cases in America forty eight resulted in disaster where people could not walk. This news devastated my parents and on the next scheduled church service they asked the church to ban together and pray for healing concerning my back. For two solid days the church prayed, and they were trusting God to do a miracle for me. Three days after my parents received this news they went back for more tests but this time the results were much different. The tests were run, and the doctor stood there in amazement as he told my parents that my back corrected itself and I would be ok.

My parents left that visit praising God and tears of gratitude ran down their faces for the power God displayed on that day. Since then I've had other accidents with my back, but God has kept me walking and leaping and praising God. All my life I've worked physical jobs, played physical sports, and have not had any restrictions whatsoever.

Without prayer I would not be walking today, and life would be much different. The Bible says in James 5:16, "The effectual fervent prayer of a righteous man availeth much". It's amazing what God can do when we pray and there would be many more healings if people prayed more often. My back was completely healed and every day I'm thankful for it. What an awesome God we have.

Scriptures For This Chapter

Luke 3:5 Every valley shall be filled, and every mountain and hill shall be brought low; and the crooked shall be made straight, and the rough ways shall be made smooth.

James 5:16 The effectual fervent prayer of a righteous man availeth much.

ANTHONY RITTHALER

CHAPTER 9

A MIRACLE THAT LEFT EVERYONE SPEECHLESS

There is nothing in this world quite like when God performs a miracle that cannot be explained away. The God we serve can raise the dead, walk on water, heal the sick, and make the impossible possible. All throughout the course of history God's miracles have changed hearts, salvaged lives, and kept untold multitudes from danger.

God will often dispatch angels whenever he feels it's necessary and when he does lives are blessed because of it. The Bible says in Psalm 91:11, "For He shall give His angels charge over thee, to keep thee in all thy ways". Over and over throughout the Bible we read of angels surprising people by their presence and every time it happens it's a humbling experience. Many around this world have had the joy of meeting them and sometimes you clearly knew while other times they pass by without your knowledge. The Bible says in Hebrews 13:2, "Be not forgetful to entertain strangers, for there by some have entertained angels unaware." I've been lucky enough to meet a handful in my life but I'm sure many have passed by me as well. I'm truly thankful for God's Divine grace and mercy and this next story will always be remarkable to me. Allow God to bless you through this amazing moment in my life.

While coming home one day I came to a four-way stop and an officer was at one of the stops. As I went to make a right turn I was hit by a car that was going forty miles per hour and it rocked my little Cobalt and it scared my daughter half to death. My daughter, Hope, started crying so I tried everything to calm her down and I made sure she was ok. My first reaction was to pull over to the side of the road to access the damage so I could give my wife the bad news. When I got out of the car the officer and woman involved were shaking their heads in amazement. As I started looking at both cars I was stunned over the fact that there was not one mark, bump, scratch, dent, or any damage whatsoever on either vehicle. She was stunned, I was stunned, and the officer more than anyone was stunned that day. None of us could believe our eyes and before I left I looked up into Heaven and marveled over what God just did.

It's hard to believe that a car could be hit at such a high speed and have no scars to show but when God is on the scene anything is possible. The Bible says, "With men this is impossible but with God all things are possible". Every time I think back on this story it still blesses me. What a loving God we have.

Scriptures For This Chapter

1 Corinthians 13: 11 When I was a child, I spake like a child, I thought as a child: but when I became a man I put away childish things.

Psalm 145:8 The Lord is gracious and full of compassion: slow to anger, and of great mercy.

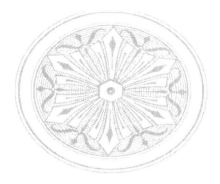

CHAPTER 10

A STEP BETWEEN ME AND DEATH

The Word of God teaches in Samuel 20:3 that "There is a step between me and death". Around this world on a daily basis roughly one hundred and fifty to one hundred and fifty five thousand people take their last breath, and God's Word declares that the wages of sin is death. The Bible says in James 4:14, "Life is but a vapor that appeareth for a little time, and then vanisheth away". God in Heaven controls our heart beats, the weather, and ultimately, he is in control of every breath we take.

Without God we can do nothing and to think you will live forever is foolish beyond measure. We have no control over when we will leave this earth and at any moment our lives can be ended if God chooses to do so. The Bible says in Laminations 3: 22-23, "It is of the Lord's mercies that we are not consumed, because His compassions fail not. They are new every morning: Great is thy faithfulness". Without God's tender mercies and amazing grace, we would be dead in trespasses and sins. We are not promised tomorrow and if you are alive today it's just because God is allowing it to happen. There is a step between me and death and the following story will prove it.

Around ten years ago after work I decided to go golfing in spite of bad weather coming in. Nothing was going to stop me, and I was determined to get a round in before it got dark. On that particular day I was shooting the best round of my life and was enjoying every second of it. As I finished hole eight the thunder began to sound but my mind was made up and I was going to finish no matter how bad it got. I remember standing on hole nine, my last Hole of the day, looking down the fairway when suddenly lightning struck the tree five feet from me and a huge branch fell to the ground. When this happened, I was holding a metal club and it could have very well been me who was hit that day.

Literally, I stood 5 feet from death that day and I am humbled that God Almighty spared my life. Always remember without God's grace life can change in a heartbeat. Make sure you are prepared to meet your God.

Scriptures For This Chapter

Psalm 91:11 For He shall give His angels charge over thee and keep thee in all thy ways.

ANTHONY RITTHALER

CHAPTER 11

A WAKE-UP CALL FROM ABOVE

The Bible talks much about the importance of waking-up out of our dead state of life and serving Him with all our might. Often in life, God ordains wake-up call moments that grab our attention, so we will be aware of how precious our time on earth is. The Bible says in Romans 13:11, "And that, knowing the time, that now it is high time to awake out of sleep". Far too many people just wander through life like zombies with no purpose, no goals, and no dreams so God Above sends events that get our attention; moments that stand out in our minds and causes us to either choose the narrow path to God or the broad way to destruction. These moments can shape our lives and cause us to become serious about eternity like we never have before. The story you are about to read was one of those moments for me and it had a profound impact on how I thought about life at an early age. This event in my life affected me and it showed me how short life can be. None of us are invincible and this story will prove that to

ANTHONY RITTHALER

us. Allow this story to minster to your heart.

Years ago, my family and I went to Cedar Point and we were having a blast. We were young, fearless, and wanted to ride every ride at the Park. Never before that day did death ever cross my mind but for the first time in my young life it did because of what I witnessed with my very own eyes.

As my brother Bobby and I were trying to decide what ride to go on next we noticed a new ride and it was called the rip cord. This ride was drawing my brother like a magnet but I had no desire to ride it, so we passed on riding it that day. The rip cord was basically a bungy cord where people were tied to a rope and dropped from a high distance. When the ride opened up people were lined up with excitement to experience this new ride but sadly that joy turned into sadness in a heartbeat. When the rope was let go 4 people hit the pavement because the rope was to long and it cost them their lives. If me and my brother would have ridden that ride that day there was a good chance we never would have made it home alive,

This was a huge wake-up call for me and when this happened Heaven and Hell became much more real that day. The Bible says in Proverbs 14:12, "There is a way that seemeth right unto a man: But the end thereof are the ways of death". God's mercy was real that day and without His grace I would not be here today. We should thank God for many things; but Him keeping us safe should be at the top of our list.

Scriptures For This Chapter

I Samuel 20:3 There is a step between me and death.

James 4:14 Life is but a vapor that appeareth for a little time, and then vanisheth away.

ANTHONY RITTHALER

CHAPTER 12

GOD SENDING GRACE DEPSITE MY FOOLISHNESS

When we are young we all tend to do foolish things we wish we could change. Moments where as adults we look back on and say, "Why did I do that"? We can either learn from these circumstances or live in regret and shame. My desire has always been to learn from mistakes and try to never repeat them again. The Bible says in Corinthians13:11, "When I was a child, I spake like a child: but when I became a man, put away childish things". It's never healthy as a person to dwell on the past unless it's used to make you a better person and it causes you to focus on grace. This next story happened as a teen and it nearly took another life and would have caused me a lot of guilt. I praise God that the Lord chose to show grace toward me and this other person and I'm thankful he spared us from a fatal mistake. Allow this next story to speak to you and show you the value of grace like it did for me that day.

May God use it to save us from making foolish decisions that can be avoided.

One day as a young man I had a burning desire to go to the driving range to hit golf balls. When I arrived that day, it was cold and windy, and I was the only one on the range. As I was hitting balls I saw the man driving the machine to pick up the balls, so I decided to try to hit the ball picker. The man driving the machine was protected everywhere except his head and I chose to hit balls at him from about 100 yards away. On that day I was hitting laser-like shots and one shot went straight through a tiny opening half an inch from his head and I saw it go through the machine he was driving to the other side. If that would have hit him it would have surely killed him, and both our lives would have been totally different. In a moment of grace from Above both his life was spared and my mind was saved from a life of regret and shame.

God's grace was real that day and I made a decision to never do something like that again. It was a turning point for me and I praise God for the great lesson I learned that day. Sometimes in our foolishness God still chooses to show compassion. We serve a God of mercy and grace and it's very clear in all our lives on a daily basis. Lamentations 3: 21-22 says "It is of the Lord's mercies that we are not consumed, because His compassions fail not. They are new every morning: Great is thy faithfulness". Thank the Lord for the grace that he offers in our foolishness. The Lord is so precious.

Scriptures For This Chapter

Romans 13:11 And that, knowing the time, that now it is high time to awake out of a sleep.

Proverbs 14:12 There is a way that seemeth right unto a man: but the end thereof are the ways of death.

CHAPTER 13

AN EYE OPENING EXPERIENCE

Working road construction often presents dangerous moments that open your eyes to death in a hurry. There is no way on earth I could explain just how many close calls I have had but I assure you it has been many. On a daily basis death stares you in the face and if you don't have a nearness to Christ fear will overwhelm you. The Bible says, "Yea I walk through the valley of the shadow of death, I will fear no evil." Often through the years while working on the road I could literally feel people praying and I could also sense angels nearby. Hebrews 13:2 says, "Be not forgetful to entertain strangers: for thereby some have entertained angels unaware".

I've seen so many amazing things in my years working construction and without God's presence close by I would have never made it out alive. This next story is awesome and it no doubt woke me up on an early Monday morning. Please allow this story of God's amazing grace to minister to you once again.

Late one Sunday night I was notified that I would be working very early on a Monday morning and I needed to be at the shop at 4:00AM. Our destination that morning was in Ohio and the work was very dangerous. Our job was to put out barrels on the side of the freeway and my job was to hang on the side of the trailer and stretch the barrel as far as I could without getting off the trailer, so the driver would not have to stop. As I was placing the barrels out cars were racing by and to be honest I was about to get a big wake-up call.

About 20 minutes into the job I reached as far as I could and from out of nowhere a semi-truck traveling at seventy miles per hour took the barrel out of my hand and I could hear the barrel dragging under his truck for about a mile. If I would not have moved my hand and body at the perfect time it could have been me and the barrel under the semi. God gave me the awareness to move at the right time and because of God's mercy I'm still here today.

The only thing that holds back death is the strong hand of Jesus. There is a great chance I could have lost my right hand or even my life that day, but God said, "My grace is sufficient for thee". Where would we be without the wonderful love of Almighty God? Every day with Jesus is sweeter than the day before and I left that day praising Him for His watchful care like I never have before. God is so good and gracious to us all, and I'll never forget what He did for me that day.

Scriptures For This Chapter

Amos 4:12 Therefore this will I do unto thee: O Israel: and because I will do this unto thee, prepare to meet thy God.

Psalm 119:73 Thy hands made me and fashioned me: give me understanding, that I may learn thy commandments.

ANTHONY RITTHALER

CHAPTER 14

GOD SENDING ANGELS AROUND US

The blessed Word of God is clear that children have guardian angels watching over them and those who fear God do too. Psalm 34:7 says, "The angel of the Lord encampeth round about them that fear Him, and delivereth them". God sends his angels from Above to set up shop around those who respect and fear Him.

The Lord has seen fit to protect me and watch over me because every where I go I'm careful about how I act and I'm mindful that a Holy God's eyes are upon me. God will always send relief to anyone who honors Him with their life and He will send protection on their behalf. This next story amazes me, blesses me, and humbles me to the lowest degree. I'll always be thankful for his watch care on that day and it shall never leave my mind by God's grace. It's great to know that God is ever near us and I pray this story blesses you in a marvelous way.

Not long ago my family and I took a much-needed vacation to Hillsdale, Michigan and we had a blast. The weather was awesome and my precious daughter, Hope, fell in love with the four-wheeler that week and it was fun driving her around. All that week was great and before we left Hope asked me to ride her on the four-wheeler one last time so that's what we did. We got on the four-wheeler and Hope said, "Can we go faster?" and I said, "Yes, but hold on tight". Hope then said, "Faster, Dad, faster" so I increased the speed to about 45MPH. As we began to go faster I realized that I was running out of land so in a split second I slammed on the brakes and when I did Hope flew through the air and hit the ground. To my amazement when she fell it was like she landed on a pillow and she asked if we could ride again.

She had no scars, hurt, or effects from the fall and God's power filled the air. Angels were around, and I could sense it. As long as I live I will always recall the grace God showed on both of us and I'll forever praise His Holy name. Psalm 150:6 says, "Let everything that hath breath praise the Lord" and that's what I was doing that day. God's eyes are upon us all and we must never forget that".

Scriptures For This Chapter

Psalm 23:4 Yea, though I walk through the valley of the shadow of death, I will fear no evil: for Thou art with me; thy rod and thy staff they comfort me.

Hebrews 13:2 Be not forgetful to entertain strangers: for thereby some have entertained angels unaware.

ANTHONY RITTHALER

CHAPTER 15

THE STRONG HAND OF GOD HELPING ME IN THE ICY CONDITIONS

It's an overwhelming and powerful thing when God's strong hand is manifested in the believer's life. The Bible says in Psalm 136:12 that, "God has a strong hand, and an outstretched arm". God is always ready at any given time to show His strength to mankind and there is no strength like His. The Bible says in Psalm 8:3 that, "The Heavens, moon, and stars were a result of the fingers of God's hand". Folks, that's a powerful and infinite God who can do that. The Bible says in Isaiah 48:13 "Mine hand also hath also laid the foundation of the earth".

No human can grasp just how strong and mighty God's hand is but with one touch the blind can see and the deaf can hear. We serve a supernatural God that can perform endless miracles and His abilities are never limited. The next story is just a small sample size of just how strong God is and I pray it brings honor to the Lamb who sitteth upon the throne.

Around nine glorious years ago I got engaged to my wife and every night I was over her house spending time with her and it was such a blessing. Back in those days I was working long hours and I was worn out but no matter how I felt I would make my way over to her house because I was in love.

My car at the time was a 2005 mustang and it was impossible to stop if the roads became icy. One night as I was driving back from Erin's house I hit black ice and my car picked up speed and was going towards the overpass. Like a magnet it struck the wall but instead of flipping over I felt a force holding my car in place and it was no doubt God Almighty. When I got out of my car to look at the damage I realized that if my car would have gone over that wall I would have fallen about 100 feet onto the highway below. God's grace was there that night and once again he showed compassion towards this unworthy creature.

The Bible says in Job 12:10, "In whose hand is the soul of every living thing; and the breadth of all mankind". I'm thankful that He holds me in the palm of His hand, and I am His and He is mine. John 10:28 says, "And I give unto them eternal life; and they shall never perish, neither shall any man pluck them out of the Father's hand". The safest place we can be is in the palm of God Almighty's strong hand.

Scriptures For This Chapter

Psalm 34:7 The angel of the Lord encampeth round about them that fear Him, and delivereth them.

Psalm 150:6 Let everything that hath breath praise the Lord.

ANTHONY RITTHALER

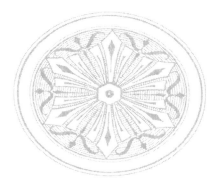

CHAPTER 16

GOD BLESSING OUR HOUSE WITH HIS GRACE

On several different occasions already, God's presence has stepped foot on our property and it has meant the world to us. We have not had our new house very long, but God's amazing grace has been rich and real, and it's brought us to our knees in thankfulness and praise. Feeling God's presence at anytime is amazing but feeling Him at God's house and your own house is the best feeling in the world.

When we went to sell our condo in Canton we had two different interested buyers. Both people as they were looking around the condo stopped and said I can feel God's presence in this home and it's strong. There is nothing that can compare to God's Spirit and when He shows up on the scene great things will happen. The next story is breathtaking, and God did a great miracle on my property. This story will bless, thrill and humble you as it did us. As you read allow God to sweep over your soul and realize if

He can do this for me He can do it for you.

After we moved into our new home in Romulus Michigan everything looked great except our roof and it was a need that had to be fixed.

We were fortunate to walk away with about eight thousand dollars spending money from the sale of our condo, so the roof was our number one concern. Immediately I contacted a friend of mine about the roof, so he gathered a team of workers and they got busy about fixing it. In around 4 days they were done, and everything was great except for the fact that they forgot to put the sealer on so it would block the rain from getting under the shingles and avoid destruction of the roof. My friend notified me of what happened, and he said Monday after work he would come over and finish the work.

Well, Monday arrived and suddenly a storm arose that brought around 3 to 4 inches of rain in my area and there was nothing I could do but pray God would hover over my property. My friend could not get there in time but thank God the Lord was there already keeping my new roof safe. That afternoon it rained extremely hard all around my house but not one single drop fell in my yard. My mother was there that day watching my daughter and she said it looked like a hand from the sky was holding back the rain. For over 40 minutes rain pounded my area but nothing touched my roof. Folks, all I can say is grace is a beautiful thing and God is a prayer answering God.

The Bible says, "The clouds are nothing more than the dust of His feet". Jeremiah 33:3 says, "Call unto Me and I will answer thee" and I am glad to report he did that day. Miracles still happen and I'm living proof of that.

Scriptures For This Chapter

Psalm 8:3 When I consider thy Heavens, the work of thy fingers, the moon, the stars, which Thou hast ordained.

Isaiah 48:13 Mine hand hath also laid the foundation of the earth.

Job 12:10 In whose hand is the soul of every living thing; and the breadth of all mankind.

ANTHONY RITTHALER

CHAPTER 17

A MIRACLE RIGHT BEFORE MY EYES

There is nothing like witnessing a miracle right before your eyes and when it happens you never forget it. Miracles come in many forms and fashions and every one of them is a gift from Heaven's shore. The Word of God says that, "With men this is impossible but with God all things are possible" and when it comes to God's miracles there are no limits to what He can do. The Lord is gracious to mankind and He is super gracious to those who fear Him.

I'll never get tired of watching God perform miracles and this next miracle left me speechless. Let me tell you what happened. Around 4 years ago as I was going to work the weather turned dangerous and the roads were a sheet of ice. There were accidents everywhere and many were slipping and sliding all over the place. Normally it would take me fifteen minutes to get to work but, on this day, it took me 45 minutes. The driving conditions were horrible, and I was just praying I could make it to work alive.

I remember being stopped by a red light just a minute from my work and I was waiting for it to turn green, so I could arrive at work safe and sound. When the light finally turned green I happened to look over to my right and a car was flying towards me and it seemed destined to hit me, but God performed a miracle for me. To my amazement the car stopped on a dime at 50MPH and it was heading right at me. There is no way that car could have stopped in those conditions unless God stopped it for me. We both had a stunned look on our faces because he knew, and I knew that what just happened was a miracle.

The Bible says in Psalm 89:52, "Blessed be the Lord for evermore Amen and Amen". If it was not for the Lord shielding us from harm where would we be ladies and gentlemen? God's mercy endureth forever.

Scriptures For This Chapter

I Peter 5:7 Casting all your care upon Him: for He careth for you.

Titus 2:11 For the grace of God that bringeth salvation hath appeared to all men.

CHAPTER 18

ALMOST DROWNING AS A YOUNG BOY

The Bible says in Psalm 118:24, "This is the day which the Lord hath made: We will rejoice and be glad in it". Everyday is meant to be appreciated and viewed as a gift from God and we are expected to make them count. Life is not a guarantee to anyone and the Bible describes it as a vapor that vanisheth away. Death can arrive at any given moment and without God's grace it can suddenly snuff out our lives.

When I was in high school I lost a dear friend who drowned and it totally shocked me. My friend was in amazing shape and he was the last person on earth who I thought that could happen to. His funeral was extremely sad and I remember his dear mother saying over and over, "not my baby, not my baby".

This moment in time brought me back to when I was a child and almost drowned as well. My dear mother rescued me just in the nick of time and I often wonder why God shed His grace upon me that day. What I learned from my friend drowning and me almost drowning is God has a reason for everything He does. My friend's funeral was sad but on the other hand many were brought to the reality of God and death and I could tell for many it was the first time.

My experience was a turning point for me and it caused me to understand that we are not promised tomorrow so we must affect lives today. God does things for one Divine purpose and that is to get people thinking about eternity. I'm thankful for God sparing my life and I use my friend's death as a motivating tool to get me serious about reaching others. Mark 8:36 says, "What shall it profit a man if he gains the whole world and loses his own soul".

If God has kept you alive there is a reason why. Let's thank God for grace and let's use the grace He has given unto us to help others. Never take life for granted ladies and gentlemen and let's cherish every day we have.

Scriptures For This Chapter

Jeremiah 33:3 Call unto me and I will answer thee: and show thee great and mighty things, which thou knowest not.

CHAPTER 19

MY CAR GETTING CAVED IN AT A BOWLING PLACE

I've learned through the years that accidents will happen and we will suffer the loss of many things but if we can come out of these things with a clean bill of health we are blessed. Things can always be replaced but life cannot be replaced. Often through our time on earth we shall suffer loss but its how we adjust to these losses that will define how we grow as people.

The Bible says that the trail of our faith worketh patience and if we handle it right we can come forth as gold. There will be ups and downs in life but the Bible says God's grace is sufficient and it will carry us through anything. The next story was shocking to witness but now, years later, I look back on it and praise God I avoided injury of any kind. We are serving a gracious God who sees the future and will direct us away from harm. Let me tell you what happened.

Years ago, my brother and I went golfing and afterwards we went into a bowling place to play an arcade game and we heard a loud bang. When we went outside to see what happened we discovered that a young man crashed into the side of my S-10 pick-up and the damage was vast. My front door was caved in and glass was all over my front seat and it would have probably killed me. I remember being stunned by what happened but instantly forgiving this young man and going on with my life.

God is good because he removed me from harm and seconds later this tragedy happened. God is a merciful and all knowing Savior . God knew what he was doing that day like He does every day and the truck was fixed and I drove it for a few more years. I'm thankful that He watched over me that day and it's just another display of his grace.

Scriptures For This Chapter

Psalm 118:24 This is the day that the Lord hath made; we will rejoice and be glad in it.

Mark 8:36 What shall it profit a man if he gains the whole world and loses his own soul.

ANTHONY RITTHALER

CHAPTER 20

IT WAS LIKE A SCENE FROM A MOVIE AND THE ANGELS PLAYED THE LEADING ROLE

Whether people fully understand it or not there are angels and they surround planet earth. God has created them, and they have many unique purposes and one of these purposes is for them to protect God's servants. If God would open our eyes to this reality most of us would fall backwards in shock over how many really exist. The next story was so amazing to witness and Hollywood on its best day could not simulate what I saw that day.

You just had to be there to fully appreciate what happened and God's power was near us all. Allow God to open your eyes through this story of grace.

As we were working on Southfield Freeway an accident took place that was staggering and intense. A semi clipped a car and spun it out of control and from there on car after car was brought into the mix and eight cars in total were involved. The noises and sounds were loud and in a moment's time cars were scattered all over the place including our company truck.

When the smoke cleared not one single person was harmed in any way; no injuries and the whole atmosphere changed as angels were sensed around us. Even lost people could not believe what just took place because it was amazing. It was probably the worst accident I ever saw, and God sent His angels to protect us that day. The scene was a disaster and a lot of clean-up was involved but God spared many souls that afternoon and His grace was poured out on us all.

Years later, I'm still in awe over what took place on that hot summer day. God has sheltered me with His love and protection all my life and I'll praise Him till the day I die. Ephesians 2:4 says, "But God who is rich in mercy for His great love wherewith He loved us". God's mercy is rich and full, and it's poured out over every one of us daily. We will never deserve His grace but every day we enjoy it. Thanks be to God, for the great things he hath done.

Scriptures For This Chapter

II Corinthians 12:9 And he said unto me, My grace is sufficient for thee; for my strength is made perfect in weakness.

Psalm 96:4 For the Lord is great, and greatly to be praised. He is to be feared above all gods.

ANTHONY RITTHALER

CHAPTER 21

WALKING ON AIR IN ALABAMA

When I was young we traveled to Alabama to visit some dear friends to bring them encouragement and support and to lift their spirits. The fellowship was sweet that entire week and we did many activities. Among those activities was climbing up a high mountain and I was very nervous about doing it. Back in those days I was deeply afraid of heights and climbing a mountain was probably last on my list but for my friends' sake I agreed to do it. As I stood at the bottom of the mountain looking up my knees became weak and fear started to fill my heart.

Just prior to starting the climb I prayed for help because I didn't want to fall off. We started our climb and the higher we got the more uncomfortable I became. About half way up the mountain I went to go take a step and I felt air under my feet and my body weight nearly carried me over the mountain and I would not be here today. Although no human rescued me that day I believe God in His grace held me up. We eventually made it to the top and I felt such a relief that I made it to the top alive.

I've never again climbed another mountain physically but now I try to climb them spiritually. Walking on air was not my cup of tea and without God holding my hand on that mountain my life would have ended that day. Jude 24 says, "Now unto Him that is able to keep you from falling and to present you faultless before the presence of His glory with exceeding joy". God fulfilled that verse on that day and he kept me from falling and he continues to do so every day.

I'm thankful for the verse in Hebrews 13:5 that says, "I will never leave thee nor forsake thee". It's great to know that when we begin to fall we have a God that can rescue us in our time of need. The God of the mountain is still God in the valley and He is a friend that sticketh closer than a brother. I'm thankful my life did not end there, and I'm determined to walk with the Lord daily in total surrender to Him. He is worthy of all praise and honor and like David I can say my cup runneth over. O what a Savior we serve and oh what a friend he is.

Scriptures For This Chapter

Jude 24 Now unto Him that is able to keep you from falling and to present you faultless before the presence of His glory with exceeding joy.

Hebrews 13:5 I will never leave thee nor forsake thee.

CHAPTER 22

GOD SHOWING MERCY AND GRACE YET AGAIN

The Bible teaches that God's mercy is ever near God's own. Psalm 136 talks about God's mercy and how wonderful it is in every verse in the chapter. God wanted to make it abundantly clear that no matter what storm we encounter it will be no match for God's amazing grace.

Everywhere we go in life God's watchful eye follows us and His grace and mercy does as well. It's a great feeling to know that we have a God that cares for us and overwhelms us with His mercy on a daily basis. The next story is a great example of grace and mercy in the way of protection that God showed for me on a hot summer day. Please enjoy this scary, yet amazing story.

One day while working road construction in Ann Arbor Michigan God poured out His mercy on me in the form of safety that was a blessing to me. My job that day was to stand on the back of the truck and place tires on barrels and kick them off the truck as it moved at about 25

MPH. The truck was raised off the ground about 10 feet in the air and in the process of working my foot slipped and I fell off a moving truck and I fell to the pavement. When I hit the pavement, God seemed to lessen the impact for me and instead of heading to the hospital I jumped back on the truck without any injury. The driver was amazed, I was amazed, and God's grace was very much real once again.

We have a God that is able to provide safety to His Saints and I stand here in amazement by His abilities every day. He truly is amazing in every single way.

I'll end this chapter with Isaiah 43:2, "When thou passeth through the waters, I will be with thee: and through the rivers they shall not overflow thee: when thou walketh through the fire, thou shalt not be burned: neither shall the flame kindle upon thee.

Scriptures For This Chapter

Psalm 37:23 The steps of a good man are ordered by the Lord.

Psalm 40:17 But I am poor and needy yet the Lord thinketh upon me: Thou art my help and my Deliverer: make no tarrying O my Go

ANTHONY RITTHALER

CHAPTER 23

GRACE WILL LEAD ME HOME

The song, "Amazing Grace", has probably had the greatest impact for the cause of Christ than any song that's ever been written. Every note of this beautiful song was written from personal experience and it seems to connect with all who hear it in some way. The third verse of this song reads like this, "Through many dangerous toils and snares I have already come, Tis grace that brought me safe thus far and grace will lead me home". This powerful verse has proven true for so many through the years including myself and without His grace we would all be a mess. The phrase, "grace will lead me home" speaks to my heart because there is no greater security then to be at home in familiar surroundings. It is grace that makes this possible and one day grace will lead to our Home on High.

This next story will shine a light on God's amazing grace and without it we would have never made it home on this particular day. May this story bring honor to the Lord and prove that prayer is the key that unlocks the door of grace in all our lives.

Around a year ago we spent an awesome week in Pigeon Forge, Tennessee that was a joy for the entire family. It refreshed our spirits and provided many memories that will stick with us forever but at week's end we were ready to come home. As we were packing to leave I got on my knees and asked God for safety on the way home and the Lord heard my prayer. As we hit the road God was near us and He sheltered us from certain disaster.

Around 15 minutes into our journey home a car started drifting into our lane and it just kept coming. As I looked over at the car it looked like a force of some kind was holding it back and eventually it drifted back into its lane. Around 30 minutes later a truck swerved in front of us and once again God's mercy caused us to avoid disaster for the second time in less than an hour.

Eventually we made it home safe and sound to Michigan and I believe without prayer this would not have been possible. God's loving kindness guided us home and His grace was shed on us that day. The Bible says, "Cast your care upon Him for He careth for you". We have a Savior that cares for us more than we will ever be able to comprehend.

Scriptures For This Chapter

Isaiah 43:2 When thou passeth through the waters, I will be with thee: and through the rivers they shall not overflow thee: when thou walketh through the fire, thou shalt not be burned: neither shall the flame kindle upon thee.

Psalm 136:3 O give thanks to the Lord of Lords: for His mercy endureth forever.

CHAPTER 24

IT'S NEVER SMART TO STIR UP A BEEHIVE

It's amazing how the curiosity of young boys can get others in trouble. The Bible says, "Foolishness is bound in the heart of a child" and we make so many mistakes in our youth. Always be mindful of how you choose your friends because if they are trouble makers it won't be long until they will cause you to follow their lead as well.

This next story is nuts and I can't believe it happened but I'm just glad God showed compassion on us that day. It's amazing no one was hurt and that's all due to God overlooking our foolishness. Allow me to tell you this crazy story.

When I was very young I used to hang out with a few boys down the road who were always getting in trouble. Almost everything they did was dangerous, and they loved to live life on the edge. One day in the backyard of one of these boys's house was the biggest beehive I've ever seen in my life. This beehive was bigger than a Medicine ball and untold thousands of bees lived inside. As we were playing one of the boys threw a steel rod through the beehive and it released thousands of bees and before we could react they were all around us. Complete madness broke out and bees covered the whole area. We all had hundreds of bees swarming us and it took us about forty five seconds to find shelter. To my amazement none of us were stung and it's remarkable how we made it out of there with no scars to show for it.

God directly overshadowed us that day and we learned our lesson. Why that boy did that I'll never know, but God shut the mouth of the lions for Daniel, and I believe God shut off the stingers for us. The Bible says in Romans 5:20, "But where sin abounded, grace did much more abound" and we sure were thankful it did that day.

Scriptures For This Chapter

Psalm 89:52 Blessed be the Lord for evermore Amen and Amen.

Matthew 19:26 But Jesus beheld them and said unto them, with men this is impossible; but with God all things are possible.

CHAPTER 25

THE ACCIDENT THAT NEARLY CHANGED MY LIFE

Before I was born my mother had an accident that nearly changed my life. Things could be completely different for me today if it wasn't for grace stepping in and touching my body.

At the church I grew up in there were two miracle babies that were in danger of suffering major damage but God's love changed all of that. One of those babies was myself and the other was a boy named Joseph Deller. Both of us were prayed over for days and both of us have gone on to encourage others and it's because of God's hand from Above touching us.

Let me explain why we were called miracle babies. I'll start with Joseph Deller. When Joe Deller was a child he came down with a very dangerous sickness that nearly claimed his life. His temperature was off the charts and the doctors feared he would have severe brain damage.

The church banded together and prayed for him and God showed mercy and today Joe Deller is one of the greatest violinists in America today. Every time I hear him play it thrills me and reminds me that God can do anything.

When I was a child my dear mother was riding a bike and took a hard fall on her stomach where my head was located. She went to the hospital and had X-rays done and the doctors feared for the worse. This news hit my parents hard, so they prayed along with the church and they were trusting God for a miracle. A few days later they went back to the doctors and they got the news that everything would be alright.

Now years later, Joe Deller is famous for his music and I am a 9-time author and we both have affected people all over the world. The futures of both of our lives were changed by godly prayers and God's grace. We were the last two people that many thought would accomplish greatness but with God nothing is impossible. The Bible says in Jeremiah 1:5, "Before I formed thee in the belly I knew thee; and before thou cameth forth out of the womb I sanctified thee, and I ordained thee a profit unto the Nations".

The Bible says in Psalm 139:14, "I will praise thee: for I am fearfully and wonderfully made". Everything I am today is due to love, mercy, grace and without His touch I am hopeless. God is the giver of life, and the only reason we live today is because God allows us to. Praise the Lord on High for what He has done and continues to do in my life and in the life of others.

Scriptures For This Chapter

Romans 5:20 But where sin abounded, grace did much more abound.

Daniel 6:22 My God hath sent His angels and has shut the lions' mouths.

ANTHONY RITTHALER

CHAPTER 26

A CLOSE CALL

All my life I've enjoyed sports and when I was young it was not uncommon for me to play sports for ten hours a day. Anytime you venture to play physical sports like basketball, baseball, hockey, and football, injuries are always a possibility. Throughout my youth I somehow avoided major injuries for the most part and considering how much I played that is a miracle.

We will all experience close calls in life, whether it be our health, with our family, with our driving, or some other area of our life. Times when God overshadows us through danger and brings us through it with grace and mercy that only He can supply. The next story is a blessing to me and it was a close call for me. This story is another moment where things could have been worse but thank God they weren't.

One day my brothers and I wanted to get a big football game together, so we called kids around the neighborhood to come join us. On that day we got enough to play 6 on 6 and the game was on. As we started to play I was picked to be receiver and my brother was the quarterback. Around 10 minutes into the game my brother dropped back to pass and he threw it in my direction. When I went up for the ball a man hit my legs and it flipped me over and I landed directly on my neck. When I landed on my neck time seemed to stand still and it did not look good. I remember laying there unsure if I could move but by God's grace I eventually stood to my feet. What's even more staggering is that I kept playing and everything was ok.

Many through the years have been paralyzed from the same type of fall but God had mercy on me and there's no way I could thank Him enough. The Bible says in Psalm 18:29, "For by thee I have run through a troop; and by my God have I leaped over a wall". The Bible also says, "I can do all things through Christ that strengtheneth me". With God's power we can face any storm, trail, pain, or mountain. He is a friend of all friends.

Scriptures For This Chapter

Jeremiah 1:5 Before I formed thee in the belly I knew thee; and before thou cameth forth out of the womb I sanctified thee, and I ordained thee a prophet unto the Nations.

Psalm 139:14 I will praise thee: for I am fearfully and wonderfully made.

ANTHONY RITTHALER

CHAPTER 27

ALL THINGS WORK TOGETHER FOR GOOD TO THEM THAT LOVE GOD

When Jesus told his disciples, "Let us go over unto the side", no storm was going to stop them. You see, Jesus was in control of the ship, the journey, and the weather and He was holding their hands, spiritually speaking. Jesus has the ability to help us face any storm that may arise and all it takes is His Word and any storm must cease.

God has a purpose for our life and when we are in the center of His will we can have confidence God will get us through. The next story is about a storm that arose suddenly, but I was on a mission that night and God brought me safely to the other side.

One night as me and my dear mother were driving to a revival meeting in Lansing, a storm came suddenly that pounded the area. When it struck us, I was on the freeway in the middle lane and it completely blocked my vision for over 10 minutes. As it was raining I could not see out of any window and I didn't know who was next to me, beside me, or behind me. All I could do is drive with no ability to see anything around. This went on for 10 minutes and how I didn't crash I'll never know.

We made it to the meeting and had a great time and I was able to give the preacher some gifts. God was basically driving my car and I was trusting in Him all the way. The Bible say in Proverbs 3:5-6, "Trust in the Lord with all thine heart: and lean not unto thine own understanding. In all thy ways acknowledge Him, and He shall direct thy paths". As I was driving through that storm, Romans 8:28 kept running through my mind. Romans 8:28 says, "And we know that all things work together for good to them that love God, to them who are called according to His purpose".

If you are going through a storm and you don't think you can get through just remember His promise that you will make it to the other side.

Scriptures For This Chapter

Psalm 18:29 For by thee I have run through a troop; and by my God have I leaped over a wall.

Philippians 4:13 I can do all things through Christ which strengtheneth me.

ANTHONY RITTHALER

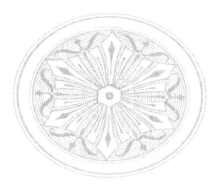

CHAPTER 28

A SHOCKING MOMENT I WAS NOT READY FOR

In life the unexpected can take us by surprise and there's nothing we can do to stop it. Moments that hit is broadside and leave us little time to react. It's during these moments that God's grace shines like never before. When things happen suddenly we are at His mercy and we need God to intervene for us.

We could all stand up and give testimonies of how God delivered is from trials we weren't expecting and there is no denying the fact that God is the very reason why. Anything can happen during these crucial moments and because of the Lord's compassion we are alive to talk about it. The following story stunned me, and it nearly caused a bad accident, but the Lord was merciful that day. Allow me to express to you what happened.

Around 6 years ago after work I made a quick decision to go golfing, so I gathered up my clubs and headed to the Throne Hills Golf Course. It was a beautiful sunny day and there was excitement in my heart about golfing and that's what filled my mind. As I got close to Throne Hills that day from out of nowhere a golf ball bounced directly in front of my truck and went right over my roof and it shocked me. When this happened, I swerved to miss it and I nearly went into a deep ditch head first.

It's not every day that a golf ball from out of nowhere bounces over your truck while driving but it happened, and it nearly caused me to crash. I was close to landing in that ditch, but God helped me gain composure over my vehicle and everything turned out ok. Psalm 136:26 "O give thanks unto the God of Heaven: for His mercy endureth forever".

I'm thankful for God helping me that day and I had a blast golfing. There is no love like the love of God.

Scriptures For This Chapter

Proverbs 3: 5-6 Trust in the Lord with all your heart: and lean not unto your own understanding. In all thine ways acknowledge Him, and He shall direct thy paths.

Romans 8:28 And we know that all things work together for good to them that love God, to them who are called according to His purpose.

CHAPTER 29

LOSING A LOT OF BLOOD THROUGH TWO CUTS AT THE GREENHOUSE IN UNDER TWO WEEKS

Whenever you lose a lot of blood it will always take a lot out of you. It's dangerous, can be fatal, and it's no fun at all.

When you are young you think you are superman and nothing can stop you but when I suffered two bad cuts in fewer than two weeks I found I wasn't as tough as I thought I was. The Bible says, "The life of the flesh is in blood", and these two major cuts made me weak and took all my energy. Let me go through both incidents and show you how rich God's grace really was.

The first incident happened as I was fixing old windows and working with old nasty glass. In the process of messing with this job, a chunk of glass broke off and cut my lip and for over two straight hours I bled. I was taken to the E.R. and became very weak and frail because so much blood was lost. That night God touched me and the next day I arrived back to work with full energy again.

Around ten days later the second incident happened, and it caused much damage too. At the end of that particular work day I was asked to close some glass windows and I followed orders. On the second to last window I closed the window but did it too hard and a piece of glass cut my head open with a deep cut and again I bled for around an hour.

In less than two weeks I bled for over three hours but in both cases I returned to work in less than twenty four hours. Both of those cuts cost me much blood, but my God's mercy brought me back to health when His touch came upon me. It's amazing how God can touch mankind and with His touch anything is possible. The mercy, love, and healing He offers never stops impressing me and without His precious blood where would we be.

Everything we are, or ever will be, is all due to the blood of Jesus. Thank God for the blood He shed on a hill called Mount Calvary. We are all so unworthy of such love and all glory goes to God above.

Scriptures For This Chapter

Psalm 136:24 O give thanks unto the God of Heaven: for his mercy endureth forever.

Psalm 145:1 I will extol thee, my God, O King: and I will bless thy name for ever and ever.

ANTHONY RITTHALER

CHAPTER 30

GOD'S PRESENCE WAS ALL AROUND

We all have moments and people along life's road that stick out in our mind whenever they are brought up or pondered upon. God brings things into our lives at different times that teach us the beauty of friendship, laughter, and His goodness in our walk with Him. Through the years I have had the joy of drawing back on precious memories of people and events that were Heaven sent and whenever I dwell on them it blesses my soul. This next story includes two wonderful Christians and just another powerful experience from God Almighty. I'm grateful to the Lord for this story and I praise Him for the presence we felt. Please enjoy this story.

When we were attending Open Door Baptist Church in Detroit, Michigan God allowed us to meet a lot of quality people that impacted our lives for Christ; men and women who were sold out to Christ and willing to give you the shirt off their back if need be. Among this great company of Christians were a couple that we built a bond with that shall never be broken. The name of this couple is Sandy and Rick Leech and words could never describe what they mean to us. Mrs. Leech is my favorite singer of all time and when she sang at Open Door tears would flow down my face and it fired me up for preaching. Bro Leach, on the other hand, had Parkinson Disease and through all his pain found ways to minister to our hearts. Every time I get around this couple I can sense God's presence and it just feels different in so many ways. We have visited the Leeches many times to be a blessing and each visit is great, but one stands out in my mind and I'll convey the details to you now.

My father called me up and said, "Son, let's go see the Leeches, I got a gift for them". So we met up and rode together. When I got in my dad's car I asked him if I could see the gift and he said sure. As I took the gift and looked at it closely I realized it was an angel figurine and I knew it was Mrs. Leech's favorite item to collect. When we got to their home we were welcomed with open arms and when my dad gave her the gift it opened up a conversation I'll never forget.

We all seemed to take turns telling of our experiences with angels and the power of God was everywhere. Tears flowed from our eyes and His glory filled that little room. As we got up to leave I took one more glance at that angel figurine and we closed that visit with prayer.

On the way home that day my dad turned to tell me something and in a blink of an eye he looked up and he was rapidly approaching a concrete wall. In a moment of desperation, he turned the steering wheel and we barely escaped a bad accident that day. Immediately after this happened Psalm 34:7 came to my mind, which says this,

"The angel of the Lord encampeth around about them that fear Him, and delivereth them". When this took place, my dad looked at me and said, "I think God may have sent His angel to protect us just now Tony".

Sometimes we fail to understand just how many angels surround us at any given moment. God is able to send one our way, but we must fear Him and walk in His ways. Thank God for His presence that day for there is no other feeling like it. The old song says, "Precious memories, how they linger, how they ever flood thy soul". And to that, I say, Amen.

Scriptures For This Chapter

Ephesians 1:7 In Him we have redemption through His blood, the forgiveness of sins, according to the riches of His grace.

Mark 9:23 Jesus said unto Him, if thou canst believe, all things are possible to him that believeth.

CHAPTER 31

WHAT A GRACIOUS GOD WE SERVE

Our God is a God of tender compassion and mercy and throughout all of our lives it is poured out in so many different ways. God takes delight in His children and if he feeds the sparrow and cares about its whereabouts, we can be sure he watches over our every move as well. Although we don't know what the future may be, I assure you that we have a God who knows what will take place years ahead of time. His knowledge and wisdom are infinite and His mercy is overwhelming.

As the devil is busy laying out stumbling blocks and pitfalls in our pathway, God longs to protect us and pour out blessings from Heaven's throne. Each and every day danger lurks but we serve a God that can lead us where we need to go. The following story is a prime example of God's mercy and I pray it will bless your heart.

Not long ago I was asked to work on a Saturday night with a man named jimmy and we were the only two working that night. At this company there is all kinds of heavy machinery and our job that night was to clean them and move them by using a big cart that did most of the work for us. On average each machine weighed about 750 to 850 pounds and we had to be extremely careful. Near the end of that night jimmy asked me to go get some cleaning supplies so that's what I did. As I was finding what I needed, I heard a loud bang and when I looked that machine fell over in the exact spot I was standing in two minutes earlier. If that machine would have fallen on me there is no way I would be here today because it would have crushed me for sure. As I looked at that machine on the ground I prayed a quick prayer thanking Him for saving my life.

The Bible says, "Be still and know that I am God" and this verse hit home that night. Folks, all I can say is that without God's grace, mercy, and love, none of us would be here today. We serve a great God that often sees fit to intervene in our lives when we need Him most. Oh, what a great God He is.

Scriptures For This Chapter

Psalm 34:7 The angel of the Lord encampeth round about them that fear Him, and delivereth them.

Psalm 33:3 He loveth righteousness and judgement: the earth is full of the goodness of the Lord.

CHAPTER 32

A MOMENT I WILL NEVER FORGET

Every day we experience is a gift from Above and we should cherish every moment we have on earth because we are not promised tomorrow. The Bible says in Proverbs 27:1, "Boast not thyself of tomorrow; for thou knowest not what a day may bring forth." No matter how great life is going today all of it can change in a split second of time and we must always be mindful of this. Every day I get out of bed I'm aware of the fact that my health, resources, family, and life, can disappear and I'm determined to be thankful for everything big and small that God gives me. James 1:17 says, "Every good gift and every perfect gift is from Above". If you have great health, praise God for that because millions around this world are not that fortunate.

God's hand of protection has overshadowed my life and all I can do is say thank you to God Almighty. Without His watch care over me I would not be here. This next moment will show you just how quick life can change.

This story proves God's grace once again and although it happened 26 years ago it's still fresh in my mind. Think about God's grace when you read about this story from my childhood.

When I was young sports consumed me and nothing thrilled me any more than playing sports with my brothers. We often played basketball, football, or baseball, for 10 hours a day and loved every second of it. When I was young I lived life on the edge sports wise and God spared me from many injuries. Out of all the injuries I avoided this moment stands out in my mind above all others.

We were at our neighbors playing baseball and I was pitching that day. My brother Bobby, was at the plate and as i delivered the pitch he hit a ball like a rocket and it hit me square in the face. When I threw the pitch I was no more than 40 ft away and it knocked my glasses off and I fell to the ground. The pitch was hit extremely hard and it could have damaged me for life but with Gods grace I stood up that day and was not hurt at all.

Gods grace is so wonderful and his compassion is endless. Anything could have happened that day, but God saw fit to show grace as he often does. He truely is a friend above all friends. Whenever I think back on moments like these, I praise God for his grace and you should too for the grace he shows towards you.

Scriptures For This Chapter

Psalm 46:10 Be still and know that I am God: I will be exalted among the heathen, I will be exalted in the earth.

Psalm 115:3 But our God is in the Heavens: He hath done whatsoever He hath pleased.

ANTHONY RITTHALER

CONCLUSION

My goal throughout this entire book was to focus on the many times where God Above stepped in and proved His awesome love, mercy, and grace in dreadful situations when hope seemed all gone. There is nothing more powerful in the world than personal experiences and I'm sure all of us could give accounts of God's amazing love because His mercies are fresh and new every morning as Lamentations 3:22 declares.

I pray you enjoyed these stories and I'm sure, as you read, your mind went back to times when God poured out mercy on you. My prayer is that God blessed you, helped you, and strengthened you through the pages of my life for I am simply a trophy of God's grace.

As I close out this book, I want to turn all the focus on what the word "grace" really stands for and why it is so amazing. As a child I learned what grace was and it has stuck with me ever since. I was taught that grace stands for God's riches at Christ's expense.

Ladies and gentlemen, Heaven is free according to Revelation 22:17 but it was not cheap for it cost Jesus His life. Christ's sacrificial death on the cross still stands as the greatest display of grace and love ever bestowed upon mankind. John said in John 15:13, "No greater love hath a man than this, that a man lay down his life for his friends". I love the old song that says, "America, America, God shed His grace on thee" and we, as Americans, take that for granted. Every day God's love surrounds us and one day this country will have to explain to God why they refused such love Divine.

Whenever you go to a football game you won't have to look far before you see John 3:16 somewhere in plain view. When you travel any distance and you look across God's great creation verses of scripture will most likely present themselves before you. There are churches on seemingly every corner, preachers within shouting distance, and general knowledge that all we see and know did not just get here by accident. As you really study what grace is, with an honest heart, tears of appreciation will flow down your face.

A dear English man took my dad out to his backyard in an attempt to present a picture of God's grace and it sticks with us forever. The old man called a lamb to his side and without kicking and fighting it came with all its innocence. The man then pulled a sharp knife out and said to my dad, "Bob, this is a picture of God's love for us, watch close". As he got ready to clearly cut the lamb's throat, the lamb looked up at his owner with eyes of love and never fought at all but rather allowed his owner to take his life. May I submit to you that when Christ died on Calvary, He was pure, innocent, and without sin, and at any time could have called 12 legions of angels to set Him free but refused out of love for us. The Bible says, "He was a lamb led to the slaughter yet He openeth not His mouth".

One of the greatest songs ever written says this, "When he was on the cross, I was on His mind". My friends, that's grace. My friends, that's love beyond human comprehension. Another song says it was not the nails that held Him there, but it was His love for you and me.

No man or woman can properly explain all the sufferings of the cross for it is impossible to understand fully. I have heard of God's love all my life and it never grows old but gets more beautiful every day. Just to think that a Holy God left it all to win a bunch of losers and vagabonds, is amazing to me.

The Bible says that Christ was the lamb slain before the foundation of the world. The Bible says that, "yet when we were without strength Christ died for the ungodly". When we weren't looking for Him, He came looking for us with arms wide open. Every day, all across the world, Christ shows grace on unworthy creatures and gives them a home in glory and so much more.

Through Grace He gives us His Spirit, His love, His blessings, eternal life, abiding victory, a clean slate, pardon, mercy, freedom, joy, all of Heaven's wonders, a new home, a new life, a new attitude, spiritual riches, a new family, and a bright future. The Bible says in Romans 8:17 that at the point of grace we become joint heirs with Christ meaning that everything he owns we will as well one day. Christ not only suffered for us, but he stands ready to bring you into His family if you repent and ask Him to forgive you of your sinful condition. The Bible says, "Where sin abounded, grace did much more abound".

I've seen God's grace change drunks, drug addicts, murderers, thieves, liars, crooks, sinners, and He can change you too. The Bible says, "The grace of God that bringeth salvation hath appeared to all men". God's grace calls out today and He is knocking on your heart's door. If you are lost you would be wise to open your heart's door and let the Savior in. If you do all the rewards of Heaven will be ushered in and you will never regret it. Don't be a fool. If God's grace appears at your hearts door swing open that door and welcome Him in gladly. The Bible teaches that God's grace is a gift, and I know from experience, it's the gift that keeps on giving.

Grace is such a wonderful thing and behind the scenes of every life is a God that longs to have a relationship with fallen men. If you have never known God's grace, don't delay any longer, come to Jesus and see what true living is all about. God can give you everything you seek and much more. There is no other word for grace but amazing.

With Love,
Bro Tony

Scriptures For This Chapter

Ephesians 2:8 for by grace are ye saved through faith; and that not of yourselves: it is the gift of God.

John 3:16 for God so loved the world, that He gave his only begotten Son, that whosoever believeth in Him should not perish, but have everlasting life.

ANTHONY RITTHALER

PUBLISHED *by* PARABLES
Earthly Stories with a Heavenly Meaning

CPSIA information can be obtained
at www.ICGtesting.com
Printed in the USA
FFOW03n0538290418
46368517-48051FF